THIS JOURNAL BELONGS TO

....

CONTACT
INFORMATION

....

....

....

DATE

....

THE *Joy*
OF THE
Lord
IS MY
Strength

JOYCE MEYER

New York • Nashville

Ellie Claire
Hachette Book Group
1290 Avenue of the Americas, New York, NY 10104
ellieclaire.com

First Edition: November 2022

Ellie Claire is a division of Hachette Book Group, Inc.

The Ellie Claire name and logo are trademarks of Hachette Book Group, Inc.

The publisher is not responsible for websites (or their content) that are not owned by the publisher.

Unless otherwise noted, the quotes in this book were taken from Joyce Meyer's books *Be Joyful* and *Strength for Each Day*.

Scripture quotations marked (NKJV) are taken from the New King James Version®. Copyright © 1982 by Thomas Nelson. Used by permission. All rights reserved.

Scripture quotations marked (NIV) are taken from the Holy Bible, New International Version®, NIV®. Copyright © 1973, 1978, 1984, 2011 by Biblica, Inc.™ Used by permission of Zondervan. All rights reserved worldwide. www.zondervan.com The "NIV" and "New International Version" are trademarks registered in the United States Patent and Trademark Office by Biblica, Inc.™

Print book interior design by Bart Dawson.

ISBN: 9781546002307

Printed in China

APS

10 9 8 7 6 5 4 3 2 1

Introduction

Truly, the joy of the Lord is our strength (Nehemiah 8:10). I am so thankful for this truth, because it teaches us that we can go through any situation knowing we are strong, confident, and victorious in Christ.

As I have said for years, joy can range from extreme hilarity to calm delight. As believers, the joy of the Lord is available to us at all times. It is a fruit of the Holy Spirit (Galatians 5:22–23), and as we live in this joy, we don't have to give in to feelings of weakness or being overwhelmed.

Sometimes joy is spontaneous. It bubbles up when something makes us happy. At other times, joy is a choice—a choice that brings hope and strength.

As you journal through these pages, I pray that you will experience the many facets of God's joy and that in every circumstance you face, you will choose to be joyful.

*D*on't let the devil steal your joy, because it is more important to you than you may think. Joy keeps you strong, and we all need strength.

Let me encourage you to take a moment to think about living in your own strength and self-effort and then about the fruit of the Spirit. You have the freedom to choose how you want to live. I have chosen to live by the Spirit, and I hope you will too.

*C*hoose today to resist negative thoughts and to think positively instead, through renewing your mind according to God's Word. The more positive your attitude is, the stronger you feel.

When we are strong inwardly, that strength often manifests in determination
that carries us through to victory in spite of many hardships.

*N*ever put off until tomorrow what needs to be changed today.
Let the Holy Spirit guide you, and take action.

God's Word does not guarantee us a life with no trials and disappointments, but it does assure us of His love and guarantees that we will never be alone.

Being obedient to God's will is the pathway to an amazing life—
a life filled with joy, peace, and every good thing.

*A*lways remember that the more time you spend receiving and abiding in God's love, the more you will be able to let it flow through you to other people.

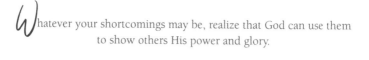

*W*hatever your shortcomings may be, realize that God can use them
to show others His power and glory.

....
....
....
....
....
....
....
....
....
....
....
....
....
....
....
....
....
....
....
....
....
....
....
....

Your worst day with Jesus will be better than your best day was without Him.

We are to be merciful toward others, just as our Father is merciful toward us. Is there anyone in your life to whom you need to extend mercy?

....
....
....
....
....
....
....
....
....
....
....
....
....
....
....
....
....
....
....
....
....
....
....
....
....
....
....
....
....
....

*While God is certainly able to change our circumstances,
He is interested in changing *us*.

When you face a challenge and you feel inadequate and weak, instead of verbalizing over and over that you are too weak, say that you are strong by declaring, "I can do all things through Christ who strengthens me" (Philippians 4:13 NKJV).

*L*earn to pray without constantly asking God to take away your problems, but ask Him to help you and those for whom you pray to endure whatever you face with patience and joy, trusting Him to ultimately bring good from it.

No matter what is on your calendar or your to-do list today, nothing is more important than your personal time with God.

I am challenging you to join me in taking every opportunity you can find to be a greater blessing everywhere you go.

Nothing is more important than your relationship with God. Keep Him first in all things, and everything else will fall into its proper place.

The more we become who God intends for us to be, the more our joy, satisfaction, and sense of purpose increase.

God is working in me and in you, and He is faithful, so don't be discouraged. Just keep believing and saying, "God is working."

God offers you grace and peace today and every day. When you live in Him, you have access to His grace and peace in every situation, which will lead you to great joy.

*L*et us forget the negative situations we have endured and focus on remembering how great our God is—and let's rehearse all of His goodness to us.

....

....

....

....

....

....

....

....

....

....

....

....

....

....

....

....

....

....

....

....

....

....

....

....

....

*S*tart your day with this positive thought—*God has blessed me today*—
and you'll find yourself more joyful all day long.

*A*s you continue to be diligent, you will reach a point in the future when you will be amazed at what God has done in you. In the meantime, enjoy where you are today!

A person may live like there is no tomorrow, but tomorrow always comes, and with it comes the harvest of the seeds we have sown in the past.

*E*xpect something good to happen *to you* and *through you.*

*L*ife does have challenges, and when we face them, being strong and stable on the inside equips us to trust God and rely on His grace in the midst of them.

*A*re you feeling guilty today about mistakes you have made in the past? If so, I encourage you to repent, receive God's forgiveness, and stop worrying about things you can do nothing about.

There is nothing better than one-on-one time with God.

*A*s God's children, we can be sure that He will never leave us. He is always with us through the Holy Spirit, allowing us to enjoy His presence.

*D*on't wait until you are out of fuel and stranded on the highway of life
before you go to God for help.

We all experience seasons of testing, times when our difficulties last longer
than we feel we can endure or when we face multiple challenges
at the same time. I encourage you to receive God's strength
while you wait on your total deliverance. He is standing by ready to help.

*I*f you concentrate on developing the fruit of love, you will also demonstrate joy, peace, patience, kindness, goodness, faithfulness, and gentleness.

*W*hatever your situation is right now, ask God for the courage you need. Believe that when He answers you, you will be greatly emboldened.

....

....

....

....

....

....

....

....

....

....

....

....

....

....

....

....

....

....

....

....

....

....

....

....

$\mathcal{G}$od will never give up on you, and no one will ever know you or love you like He does.

You cannot control what others do, but you can learn, with God's help,
not to let them control you.

God's Word will guide you, encourage you, give you wisdom, and give you
the confidence you need to face each day.

Don't worry about tomorrow, but instead enjoy today. When tomorrow dawns, you will find the grace to deal with anything that comes with it.

Being strengthened on the inside empowers us to be steadfast and stable, and one of the qualities that people in the world need to see in us is stability.

....

....

....

....

....

....

....

....

....

....

....

....

....

....

....

....

....

....

....

....

....

....

....

What battle are you fighting right now? Don't make the mistake of trying to fight it alone. God is with you, and He will help you by giving you the strength you need to stand strong while He works in your life and in your situation.

....
....
....
....
....
....
....
....
....
....
....
....
....
....
....
....
....
....
....
....
....
....
....
....

You may not be where you want to be right now in certain areas of your life, but you can be thankful that you are not where you once were. You are making progress, even if it is only a tiny bit at a time.

*E*ach day that God gives us is a gift, and if we waste it, we can never get it back and make it useful. Let God guide you, and be purposeful about how you spend your time.

When we try to carry burdens in our own strength without God's grace,
our hearts can grow heavy.

....
....
....
....
....
....
....
....
....
....
....
....
....
....
....
....
....
....
....
....
....
....
....
....

*L*et go and let God show His strength through you.

The lessons and principles you are learning today will come back to you just when you need them in the future.

*A*lways let the peace of God rule in your heart, and your life will be fulfilling rather than disappointing.

God doesn't want us to serve Him out of fear of His anger but because of our love and appreciation for all He has done and continues to do for us.

*A*nytime—and all the time—is the right time to give thanks to God, but it is especially important that we don't forget to do so while we are in the wilderness times of our lives.

....
....
....
....
....
....
....
....
....
....
....
....
....
....
....
....
....
....
....
....
....
....
....
....

*Through the power of the Holy Spirit, we can live holy, righteous lives and glorify God.
He has set us free, and He empowers us to stay free.*

The anticipation of the good things to come is part of what makes them exciting.
I urge you today to make a decision to stop being in such a hurry
and simply enjoy your journey.

....
....
....
....
....
....
....
....
....
....
....
....
....
....
....
....
....
....
....
....
....
....
....
....
....
....
....
....

Here is one great promise of God that causes me to rejoice: "And we know that in all things God works for the good of those who love him, who have been called according to his purpose" (Romans 8:28 NIV).

I believe that a meek person is one who can maintain balance between emotional extremes and manage emotions appropriately. This requires strength, not weakness. Meekness is not weakness; it is strength under control.

....

....

....

....

....

....

....

....

....

....

....

....

....

....

....

....

....

....

....

....

....

....

....

....

....

*W*ith God's help, you can remain emotionally steady when everyone else is tossed about by circumstances.

*L*et's remember that God never commands us to be busy, but to be fruitful (productive). We can be busy doing nothing, or busy doing something that will add value to our life or to someone else's.

What does it take to rejoice in the Lord? It requires thinking about what we have in Christ rather than focusing on our circumstances.

*D*o you desire greater joy? If so, I encourage you to increase your gratitude, and it will turn into joy.

*Y*ou are never left alone. You never have to do anything alone.
You are never far away from the help or the hope you need.
God is never more than one thought away from you.

I encourage you to wait patiently on the Lord today, trusting Him
to answer you when the time is right.

When you are deeply rooted in God's love and you know who you are in Christ, exercising self-control and making good choices, instead of yielding to the enemy's temptation, is not difficult.

To be confident in God is to place the full weight of our belief in Him, never doubting that He will come through for us.

*O*nly when we understand that we cannot do anything to make God love us
or accept us, and realize that we are saved and made right with
God through Christ and Him alone, can we truly live.

We all have enemies of some sort or another, but God is fighting for us. You may be going through something difficult right now, but be encouraged that God is with you and that His plan is to deliver you.

*I*f God calls you to do something, He will also provide what you need to do it—skills, finances, and, if needed, people to help you, along with other resources.

The more we know God's Word, the quicker we will recognize the lies of Satan.
If we submit to God by honoring His Word above all else,
we can then resist the devil, and he will flee from us.

With God, we don't need to pretend, hide, or make excuses.

*W*e all want the blessings of joy and peace of mind, but we will miss out on them if we meditate on every thought that comes to us without examining its source. Think about what you're thinking about.

*L*et me encourage you to get up each morning and think,
I have everything that I need to have a wonderful day.
God has already blessed me with every spiritual blessing available.

*L*et kindness rule in your home and in all your dealings with others. One of the best ways to release joy in your own life is to offer it to others through being kind to them.

*The more you keep going forward in Christ and refuse to quit,
the more spiritually strong and stable you will become.*

*I*f you are at odds with anyone at this time in your life, I urge you to forgive any offenses today and make peace with that person in obedience to God.

....
....
....
....
....
....
....
....
....
....
....
....
....
....
....
....
....
....
....
....
....
....
....
....
....

I encourage you to ask the Holy Spirit to help you to be a person who avoids strife, restores peace, and spreads joy everywhere you go.

Refuse to keep running into walls; tear them down and start making progress.

We don't please God by doing everything perfectly all the time. We please God by having faith, loving Him, and wanting to mature in Him.

Once you become aware of a sin or fault in your life, confess it to the Lord, repent, and ask for His help to overcome it. Don't focus on what is wrong with you, because in Christ, there is more right with you than there is wrong.

God has provided for us everything we need, yet we often waste years trying to obtain things that mean much less than the spiritual blessings He has already given us because we are His children.

If you need a fresh start in any area of your life, Jesus has His arms outstretched and is waiting for you to let Him help you begin again.

Receive God's mercy and love today, and let it remove all fear from your life.
Nothing can separate you from God's love, which is found
in Christ Jesus (see Romans 8:37–39).

Trust God to guide you to the next opportunity, and keep trying things until you land in the place you know in your heart that God has for you.

*L*et me encourage you today: Do not give up. Persevere through difficulties, and be patient. Keep trusting in God, and keep on keeping on!

God demonstrates His love for us through the way He treats us, and we show our love for others through the way we treat them.

....
....
....
....
....
....
....
....
....
....
....
....
....
....
....
....
....
....
....
....
....
....
....
....
....
....
....
....
....

*P*rayer opens the door to God's power and invites Him to change things and people. It opens doors you could never open, and it closes doors that would lead to something that is not good.

*L*et me encourage you today: Next time you find yourself in a tense situation, choose not to join in and make it worse. Choose instead to ask God to help you bring and keep peace.

*L*et me encourage you today to think about what steals your joy. Decide that you will not feed it anymore and that, instead, you will focus on thoughts and actions that will increase the joy that God has given you.

If you are facing trouble or difficulty today, run into God's presence. It's the safest place you'll ever find.

When God is truly leading us, we have a deep sense of peace in our hearts about the direction in which He wants us to go.

Begin each day thinking about what you believe would be good choices to make, and don't let yourself be distracted by useless things that steal your time and produce no good fruit.

Jesus paid the price for us to become spiritually alive in Him, to be completely forgiven of our sin and given a new life. He did this because He loves us.

God doesn't simply give us strength; He is our strength!

*U*se your words today to encourage others. Remember that your words
have power, so make sure they are positive and beneficial
to you and to the people in your life.

Fullness of joy is found in God's presence, not in His presents. This means we find joy in who God is and in simply being with Him, not in the things He can do for us.

*N*o matter how much Satan seeks our harm and destruction, God always has a plan for our rescue and victory. No matter what we go through, God is always aware of it and is always able to intervene.

....
....
....
....
....
....
....
....
....
....
....
....
....
....
....
....
....
....
....
....
....
....
....
....
....

*L*et's learn to see the extraordinary in ordinary, everyday life.
I can promise you it is there if you will simply look for it.

We should not do what is right simply to receive a reward, but we should do it because it is right.

If pursuing a greater lifestyle of obedience would prevent some of our problems, let's be wise and do it.

....

....

....

....

....

....

....

....

....

....

....

....

....

....

....

....

....

....

....

....

....

....

There are no limits to the ways we need God's grace, and thankfully, there is no limit to the grace God is willing to give us.

No matter what you may face today, you can choose to rejoice and to rest in God's love. He is with you and He is for you, not against you.

*D*o good intentionally, and don't grow weary of doing it!

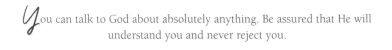

You can talk to God about absolutely anything. Be assured that He will understand you and never reject you.

We don't rejoice because we are suffering. No one enjoys suffering, but we can rejoice that we have hope through Christ in the midst of our pain and struggles.

....

....

....

....

....

....

....

....

....

....

....

....

....

....

....

....

....

....

....

....

....

....

....

....

I encourage you to make a decision to enjoy this day and every day of your life, no matter what difficulties life may bring.

God's promises never fail. Their fulfillment may take longer than we would like, but if we don't grow weary and we keep doing what is right, our reward will come.

God created you to be an original, not to compare yourself with someone else and copy them. Enjoy the unique people He has placed in your life, while giving them the chance to enjoy the unique you.

The more we realize what God has already done for us through Jesus and the more we receive it by faith, the more we are able to find real joy in each day.

Whatever battle you are facing today, take your position in praise and worship. Praising and worshiping God will strengthen you and defeat the enemy. There is real power—spiritual power—in worship.

....
....
....
....
....
....
....
....
....
....
....
....
....
....
....
....
....
....
....
....
....
....
....
....
....

Over the course of your life, certain things may change. God's will for you today may not be His will for you ten years from now, but as you continue to seek it, He will continue to reveal it.

Fear is from the devil, and it is intended to prevent you from making progress of any kind.

....

....

....

....

....

....

....

....

....

....

....

....

....

....

....

....

....

....

....

....

....

....

....

Just imagine how much better our relationships would be
if we all had Spirit-filled personalities.

....
....
....
....
....
....
....
....
....
....
....
....
....
....
....
....
....
....
....
....
....
....
....
....
....
....

*G*od is never more than one thought away from you, so think of Him often and talk with Him out loud or silently throughout your day.

If we are not stable on the inside, and if our temperament and commitment to God change constantly based on our circumstances, we don't inspire people to want to know Him. But if we remain emotionally steady through every situation, people notice.

God understands how you feel, and He cares. Don't feel you must try to hide your feelings from Him. Instead, tell Him everything and ask for His help.

*P*rayer is simply talking with God and listening to Him as we would
in a conversation with a friend.

The Lord wants to use you and all your experiences in life. You may look at your past and think, *I've wasted so many years,* but they don't have to be wasted if you gather them up and release them to God for His use.

....

....

....

....

....

....

....

....

....

....

....

....

....

....

....

....

....

....

....

....

....

....

....

....

....

....

....

....

*Y*our life before Christ may have been characterized by worry, fear, and anxiety, but now that you are in Him, you can have a life of rest, peace, and joy.

*I*f you find yourself becoming angry or bitter because you have not received the appreciation you feel you deserve, take it as a sign that you need to adjust your motive for your service to others.

We don't have to be happy about suffering, but we can choose to endure it with the joy of the Lord in our hearts. As we do, He will strengthen us and release more and more grace to carry us through it.

I encourage you today to position yourself for a great future by choosing thoughts and words that please the Lord.

*Experience tells us that unless we have thankful hearts that look for reasons
to be grateful, we will always find something to complain about,
no matter what God does for us.*

I encourage you today to enter God's rest, relax in His presence, and enjoy your relationship with Him.

*G*odly thoughts will strengthen your faith.

*S*taying in close fellowship with God is always in our best interest, so guard your heart against unforgiveness. When you feel it creeping in, deal with it quickly.

*A*nyone can be joyful when they have everything they want or when everything is going their way, but it takes the power of the Holy Spirit to remain steadfastly joyful in our hearts when we face difficulties or disappointments.

*T*he truth is that no matter what we have, it is impossible to be satisfied and content unless having it is within God's will for our lives.

When you are under an attack of worry, instead of striving hard to stop worrying, ask the Holy Spirit to help you; then hold your peace while God works in your situation.

The more we make others happy and stop trying so hard to please ourselves, the happier we will be.

$\int$ f our thoughts align with God's Word, our lives will also align with His Word—
and that is the key to blessing and joy.

With God's help, we can handle difficult situations while remaining peaceful.

The decision is up to us, but if we desire joy, we should always focus on good things.

I encourage you today to live with the expectation that God will do something amazing in your life at any moment.

Keep lifting up the truth of God's Word and let it work against
any facts that don't agree with it.

*L*et us be merciful to those around us, because when we sow mercy, we will reap mercy.

I pray often for inner strength, perhaps several times each day. I encourage you to begin to pray for inner strength also, both for yourself and for the people you love.

*W*hatever happens in your life, go to God with it first, and seek to know His will and His way to deal with it.

*L*et me remind you that our thoughts become our words, and our thoughts
and words affect our moods and attitudes.

The devil suggests doubts to us in the form of thoughts, but we don't have to ponder them or allow them to take root in our minds, making us feel confused or lost in our way.

Prayer is what changes our circumstances and our relationships,
and it also changes us.

Our Lord has a good plan for each of us, and He is daily guiding us into the fullness of that plan as we spend time in prayer and in His Word.

One of the best ways to find and maintain joy in our lives is to devote ourselves to prayer.

The source of your strength is your faith in God.

*U*pon discovering that we can give up all our striving and self-effort and have Christ and His righteousness—instead of trying to earn righteousness ourselves— a burden lifts from us, and we can begin to enjoy God and the life He has given us.

*L*earning to recognize and enjoy the presence of God is an important part of our worship of Him, and it is important for us if we want to live with peace, joy, and great courage.

....

....

....

....

....

....

....

....

....

....

....

....

....

....

....

....

....

....

....

....

....

....

....

....

....

....

....

_R_omans 15:13 changed my negative thinking and restored my faith
as I realized how important believing is!

*T*rue joy is found only in God's presence, and in serving Him according to His will.

You ou and I can also find joy in our faith. The better we know Christ,
the stronger our faith will be, and the greater our joy will be.

*W*hen you need strength, don't seek it in any worldly source. Ask God to empower you to do whatever you need to do. He will always come through for you.

....
....
....
....
....
....
....
....
....
....
....
....
....
....
....
....
....
....
....
....
....
....
....
....
....
....

I encourage you to study God's Word with enthusiasm, as though you are expecting
to find a precious Bible gem that will help you greatly.

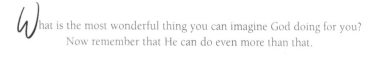

*W*hat is the most wonderful thing you can imagine God doing for you?
Now remember that He can do even more than that.

....
....
....
....
....
....
....
....
....
....
....
....
....
....
....
....
....
....
....
....
....
....
....
....
....

God loves us so much that He made the greatest sacrifice imaginable so that we could be free and forgiven and so that we could live in peace and joy. We honor Him when we embrace this gift, but we dishonor Him when we reject it.

I encourage you today to simply notice and appreciate the beauty of God's creation around you.

The more thankful we are, the more joyful we will be.

*P*eace in your soul confirms that your actions or intended actions are within God's will for you; it acts as an umpire, calling the "plays" or choices you're making as right or wrong for you.

God is never more than one thought away from us, so I encourage you to think of Him often, whisper your gratitude to Him for different things all throughout the day, and ask for His help in everything, even in seemingly insignificant things.

When we believe and speak according to God's Word, things in our lives begin to change and line up with His will and His good plan for us.

With the right mindset, a happy heart, a good attitude, and the confidence that God loves you, your inner life can be strong, peaceful, and joyful.

*T*rust that God knows every detail of your situation. Trust that He cares for you more than you can imagine. And trust that He is always working in your very best interest, even when you cannot see it.

The more joyful you are, the stronger you will be.

None of us knows what a day may hold, but we can be confident that because God helps us, we will be strong and victorious.